What would Love say?

author
Esther Dar

illustrator
Gary Wein

Copyright © 2017 Esther Dar.
All rights reserved. No part of this book may be used or reproduced by any means, graphic, electronic, or mechanical, including photocopying, recording, taping or by any information storage retrieval system without the written permission of the author except in the case of brief quotations embodied in critical articles and reviews.

Books may be ordered through booksellers or by contacting:
RED Publications
www.estherdarchildrensbooks.ca
estherdar4272@gmail.com

Because of the dynamic nature of the Internet,
any web addresses or links contained in this book may have changed since publication and may no longer be valid.
ISBN-13: 978-1979092463

To my children, Sarah, Yael, and David, and to my nephews and nieces, Naor, Adi, Ben, and Lilly, and to all of G-d's children, may you always remember you are love, you are lovable, and you are loving.

Gary would like to dedicate this book to Mina.

Acknowledgements

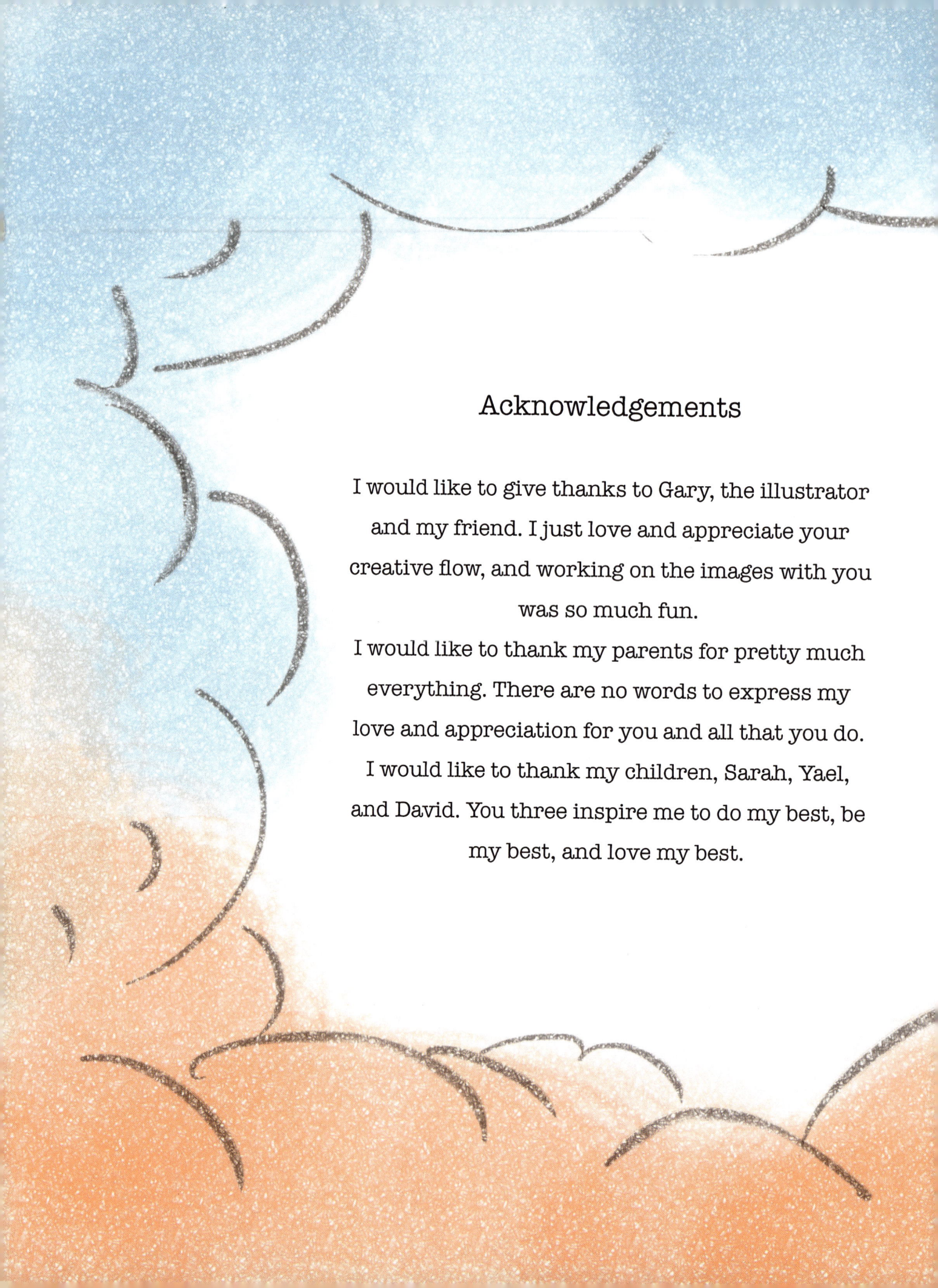

I would like to give thanks to Gary, the illustrator and my friend. I just love and appreciate your creative flow, and working on the images with you was so much fun.
I would like to thank my parents for pretty much everything. There are no words to express my love and appreciation for you and all that you do.
I would like to thank my children, Sarah, Yael, and David. You three inspire me to do my best, be my best, and love my best.

What would Love say?

Love would say, "Peekaboo, I see you, and I like what I see."

Love would say, "Have no doubt, you are beautiful inside and out."

What would Love say?

Love would say, "I am happy you are you."

Love would say, "Let me dry your tears. It's okay if you have three ears."

Love would say, "It's okay to make mistakes. Keep trying, just do what it takes."

Love would say, "Splashing in puddles with you is so much fun. Hold my hand and let's run."

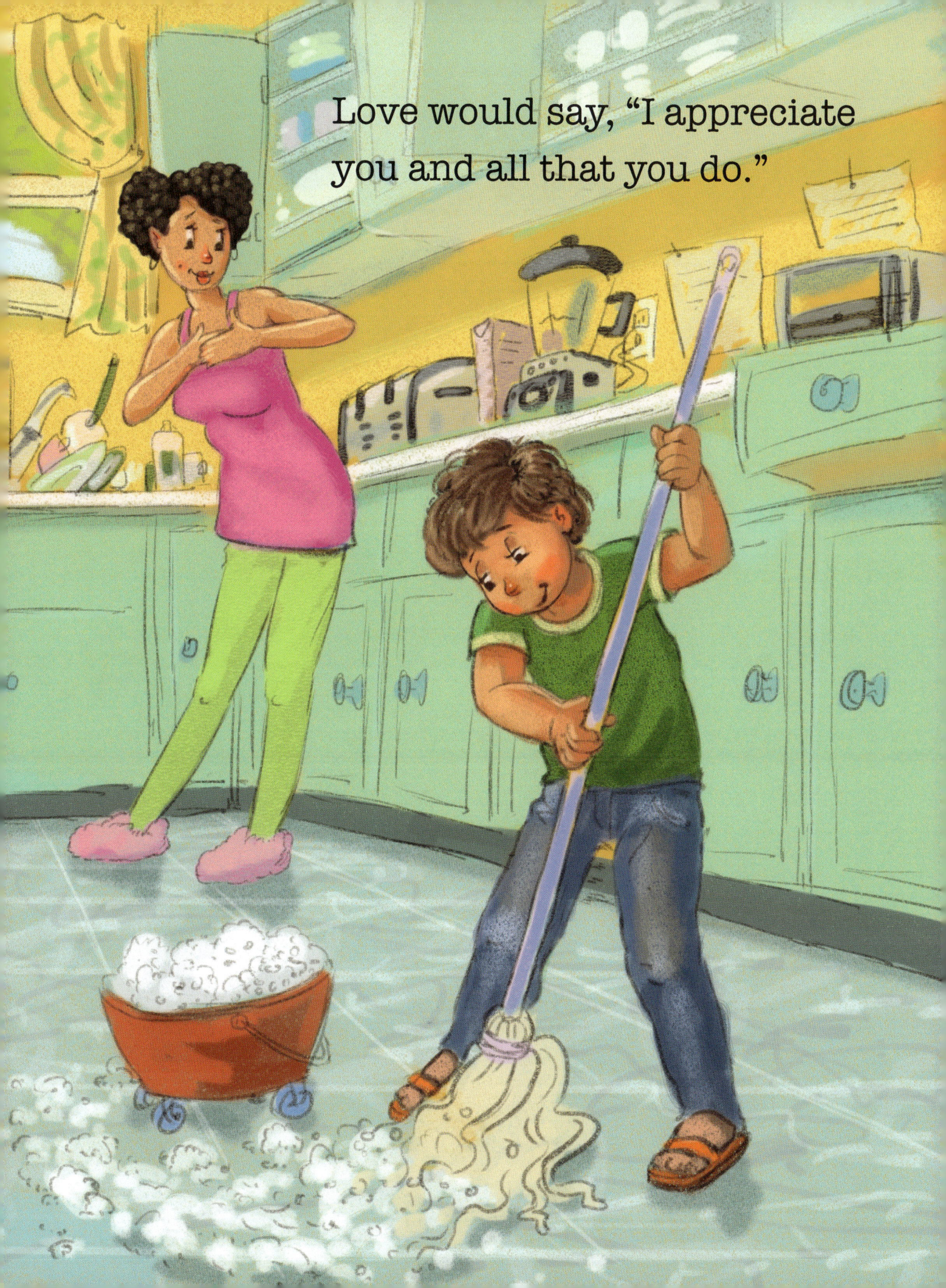

Love would say, "You're not alone. This whole, wide world is your home."

What would Love say?

Love would say, "You are so special. There is no other like you, not here, nor there, not anywhere."

Love would say, "You are loveable. I am loveable. We are lovable."

Proof

Made in the USA
Columbia, SC
24 December 2017